LIVING FOR THE *FUTURE*

TOURISM IN BALANCE

Sally Morgan

W

FRANKLIN WATTS

NEW YORK • LONDON • SYDNEY

Most of our everyday activities, whether turning on a light or taking a trip in a car, use up some of the earth's resources. These resources will not last forever, yet we continue to need and use them in our daily lives.

In June 1992, the largest ever political meeting in history was held – the United Nations Conference on Environment and Development (UNCED), or the 'Earth Summit'. Politicians, environmental experts and many others gathered together to discuss the challenge that humanity faces as we move towards the twenty-first century. How can we live our lives in a way that suits us, but without using up the resources that our children in turn will need to live their lives?

Agenda 21 is the document that was produced as a result of the Earth Summit. It sets out a practical plan for every nation to follow to achieve 'sustainable development'. This means not only allowing us to live the lives we want to lead, but allowing everyone else to live a comfortable life, while also protecting our environment for future generations.

© 1998 Franklin Watts
96 Leonard Street
London
EC2A 4RH

Franklin Watts Australia
14 Mars Road
Lane Cove
NSW 2066

ISBN 0 7496 2856 1

Dewey Decimal Classification Number 338.4

A CIP catalogue record for this book is available from the British Library

Series editor: Helen Lanz
Series designer: Kirstie Billingham
Designer: Simon Borrough
Picture research: Sue Mennell
Consultant: Niall Marriott, a founder of Living Earth Foundation and consultant in environmental, community and educational issues

Printed in the United Kingdom

Picture credits:
Cover images: Front cover Panos Pictures (Penny Tweedie) left; Rex Features right: Backcover Still Pictures (Adrian Arbib).

Interior: Bruce Coleman 6b (N. McAllister), 9, 11b (Dr. Eckart Pott), 15t (Erwin & Peggy Bauer), 17t (Andrew Davies), 19b (M. Timothy O'Keefe), 20t (Michael Klinec), 21t (Sefano Amantins), 21b (Staffan Widstrand), 22t (John Worrall), 23b (Dr. Stephen Coyne), 24t (Luiz Clandio Marigo), 24b & 25t (John Shaw), 26 (Nancy Sefton), 29t (Patrick Loertscher); Bruce Coleman/ Atlantide SDF 5tr, 9, 16b, 18, 19t; Ecoscene 12b (Jim Winkley), 14t (Ian Booth), 16m (Jim Winkley), 17b (Ian Harwood), 20b (Joel Creed), 25b (Louise Lindegger), 28t (Robert Weight); E. T. Archive/Tate Gallery 4b (Bank Holiday, Brighton by Charles Cundall, 1933); Eye Ubiquitous 22b (J. Waterlow); Panos Pictures 7t (Peter Barker), 7b (Jean-Leo Dugast), 10b (David Reed), 11t (Paul Weinberg) 12t (Nic Dunlop), 13b (Jean-Leo Dugast), 16t (Guy Mansfield), 21m (Sean Sprague); Rex Features 8b (Ben Simmons); Robert Harding 5b, 6t, 14b (Roy Rainford), 15b (Adam Woolfitt); Still Pictures 4t (J. Frebet), 5tl (Mark Carwardine), 8t (Mark Edwards), 10t (Michael Doolittle), 13t (Julio Etchart); 23t (Carlos Guarita), 24m (Mark Carwardine), 27t (Alain Compost), 27b (Thierry Thomas), 28b (Peter Frischmuth), 29b (Roland Seitre).

CONTENTS

About two thousand years ago, traders and explorers began to travel and return home with fascinating tales of strange and beautiful lands. For many centuries, only the rich could afford to travel for pleasure to see these places, but today almost everyone can go on holiday to visit different countries, learn about other cultures, or perhaps just sit in the sun. Many of us have seen exotic places on television and want to experience them in person.

Visiting the world's wonders is a popular pastime.

WHY DO WE GO ON HOLIDAY?

Brighton, in the UK, was a popular tourist spot in the 1930s.

GRAND TOURS

Amongst the earliest travellers were pilgrims who journeyed to shrines and cathedrals. By the 18th century, it became fashionable for rich people to travel through Europe on the Grand Tour. Later, people travelled to spa towns, such as Bath in the UK or Baden Baden in Germany, to 'take the waters' for health reasons. Tourist areas grew up around the spas.

'No corner of the planet is immune, however remote or inhospitable. All the world is just another destination.'

Jonathan Porritt, January 1997.

Whether visiting the beautiful Akaka Falls, on the Hawaiian Islands, or the humpback whale in its natural environment, more destinations are becoming accessible.

PACKAGE HOLIDAYS

In 1841, an Englishman called Thomas Cook started to organize day trips and then seaside holidays for groups of people. Soon he began to arrange holidays overseas. Now, a huge range of ready-made 'package holidays' can be bought through many different travel agents. All arrangements, including transport to the resort, hotels, meals and excursions are included in the price of the package. As leisure time increases and travel becomes easier and cheaper, foreign holidays will become even more popular.

People on package tours are taken from airport to hotel.

Tourism is growing rapidly and, before long, it will be the world's biggest industry. Already, one in every ten people work in tourism, that is 204 million people. This number is expected to double in the next ten years.

Guide work is usually seasonal, except at busy attractions.

TOURISM AND AGENDA 21

Increasing numbers of tourists create growing problems. More hotels, restaurants, roads and airports are needed every year. Very often, these are built on beautiful coastlines or in unspoilt countryside. Important wildlife habitats disappear under concrete. The sewage and waste generated by the tourists often ends up in the sea.

In hot, dry countries, water is in short supply and the tourist industry can create water shortages. Tourists visiting game reserves in East Africa, for example, expect water to be available for showering, even though they spend the day driving around a barren grassland in which water is scarce.

Belize is a new holiday destination. Already hotels are appearing along the once unspoilt coastline.

THE NEEDS OF THE TOURIST

Many tourists expect luxury hotels and good food, even when they are visiting poor countries. This can cause environmental damage and even food shortages for the locals.

Tourists hire cars and coaches to visit the sights, using country roads which were not built for heavy traffic. Historic towns become clogged with traffic, which causes the air to become polluted. Remote mountain streams, exotic beaches and colourful reefs have all been polluted by tourists.

In Phnom Penh, Cambodia, a luxury hotel overlooks a shanty town, where local people live in poverty.

So why do countries encourage tourists? It is simply because tourism brings in a lot of money, which helps to create local jobs.

While managed tourism is thought to be less environmentally damaging than mining, logging, or intensive farming, unmanaged tourist development can be as destructive.

People must be aware that what they do affects the environment.

AGENDA 21

In 1992, a huge conference called the Earth Summit was held in Rio de Janeiro, Brazil. Representatives from around the world gathered to discuss the future of the earth and its environment. They discussed how the world was going to continue to develop, and how we were going to maintain our lifestyles, while at the same time protecting the environment, wildlife and the earth's resources. This is called 'sustainable development'.

World leaders, including Gro Bruntland, the then Prime Minister of Norway, attended the Earth Summit in June 1992.

One hundred million people a year head for the Mediterranean, while North American National Parks receive four hundred million visitors.

One product of the summit was a document called Agenda 21. This suggests how sustainable development can be achieved by all the countries of the world.

Tourism looks set to continue into the next century. But it is vital that the industry develops in a sustainable way. The tourist trade has to strike a balance between attracting more travellers and looking after the environment.

Tour operators have to keep their customers happy by making sure that they have a good holiday. Overcrowding can spoil a resort and eventually people will choose somewhere else to go.

AGENDA 21

Here are some of the most important aims of Agenda 21 for sustainable tourism:

- respect the environment and the cultures of local people
- avoid overcrowding resorts
- make sure new resorts and hotels suit the local environment
- protect heritage sites and ancient monuments
- prevent the illegal trade in historic objects, crafts and wildlife souvenirs
- make sure that the local people benefit from tourism
- reduce waste, encourage reuse and recycling, and conserve energy
- look after supplies of fresh water and dispose of waste carefully

CASE STUDY

JAISALMER, INDIA

HOW NOT TO DO IT!

Jaisalmer, in India, is a popular destination for tourists in search of somewhere remote, unspoilt by modern life. But, as more tourists visit, the attractiveness of the town is being damaged. Jeeps take visitors to exclusive desert palaces which have been turned into four-star hotels with hot showers, imported foods and other Western 'needs'. The rubbish that is created is not disposed of carefully – paper and plastic bottles are burnt on open fires.

If this continues, the tourists will spoil Jaisalmer and no one will want to visit there any longer. Then the income from tourism that the locals have come to depend on will dry up.

Jaisalmer has very beautiful architecture which people flock to see. The number of visitors needs to be controlled, so Jaisalmer can retain its beauty.

AGENDA 21 aims to:

- encourage low impact, environmentally sensitive holidays
- avoid overcrowding
- preserve the environment
- make sure some of the profit goes to the local community
- ensure that holiday-makers respect the local culture

A tourist learns about Yagua life

ECOTOURISM— THE WAY AHEAD

During the 1980s, alternative forms of tourism started to develop. One of these alternatives is ecotourism. This is nature-based and aims to give tourists a better understanding of the country they are visiting, as well as protecting the environment. Eco-sensitive tour operators make sure that tourists look after the places they visit, and encourage people to respect local cultures.

Visitors stay in hotels built from renewable resources, such as timber. Resorts use alternative energy, such as solar and wind power. Waste water is disposed of carefully so it does not pollute the local rivers. The number of people visiting the resorts is also limited – authorities now realize it is important not to swamp a destination's resources.

Tourist accommodation can be built to blend in with the local environment, such as these chalets at Sikumi Tree Lodge in Zimbabwe.

These South African children attend a school that benefits from money raised by the local Phinda Game Reserve.

Ecotourism involves the local community as well. Far too often, the money from tourism does not benefit the locals, but merely makes money for the tour companies and airlines. If a tourist resort or national park is to be properly protected, the local community must be involved. Some of the money from tourism must be put back into the community – for building new schools and hospitals, and for creating new jobs. If the people benefit, it will be in their interest to protect the local environment – if it is spoilt they will suffer.

'Arranging and promoting meaningful contact between travellers and local people is one of our priorities.'

Costa Rican Expeditions.

CASE STUDY

LAPA RIOS, COSTA RICA

ECOTOURISM IN ACTION

Lapa Rios is a private nature reserve in Costa Rica that protects 400 hectares of the rainforest. The lodge and bungalows are built from renewable materials such as palm, bamboo and mangrove posts. No living trees were cut down to build them. Only a small number of tourists can stay at any one time, so the reserve does not get disturbed. They are taken on guided walks through the forest to learn about its wildlife and conservation. The money from tourism is spent on more conservation and helping the local villagers.

These brightly-coloured scarlet macaw are a common sight in Lapa Rios. In order that they remain so, officials must work hard to preserve the conservation area.

AGENDA **21** aims to:

- promote ways of travelling that minimize air pollution
- encourage tourists to walk or hire bikes instead of using cars

EASY TRAVEL

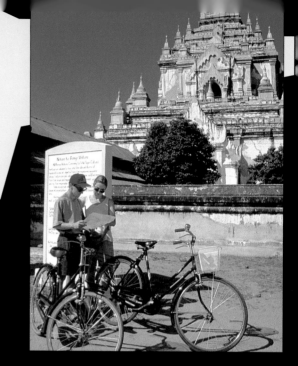

In the past, travel was difficult and people who travelled had to use trains or boats. Journeys by overland transport could take many days. Cars made travelling easier, but it is the aeroplane that has made the most impact. Nowadays, aircraft can take tourists almost anywhere in the world.

Once, faraway destinations were too expensive for most people to reach. Today, costs have fallen dramatically. Lower prices and quicker modes of transport mean that many people can now visit the other side of the world for just a two-week holiday. Once unspoilt destinations now see the arrival of hundreds of holiday-makers each week. Nowhere is out of reach, even the Antarctic. But at what cost?

As travel becomes easier, more people choose to visit more places. There are no longer many destinations in the world that people cannot reach.

POLLUTING THE AIR

Planes need fuel, which comes from oil. Oil is a non-renewable resource, that is, a resource that is running out and cannot be replaced. Also, jet engines, like car engines, create air pollution which affects the atmosphere. Scientists have found that trees which grow close to airports are dying from the air pollution.

MORE AIRPORTS

Planes need airports. As the number of planes increases, so does the number and size of airports. In some countries, where land is in short supply, airport runways are built on man-made islands, made from gravel and concrete. This affects the marine environment, polluting the nearby waters and coral reefs.

Hong Kong is already overcrowded. To accommodate a new airport, a new island was built and much marine life was lost.

Large airports, such as Heathrow in London, have to expand to meet the needs of more travel. New terminals are built to handle the extra tourists, and new runways laid down for the extra planes. As airports expand important wildlife habitats are lost. The local communities have to suffer more noise, air pollution and traffic, both in the air and on the roads.

One way forward may be to charge tourists an airport tax, which could be used to fund conservation in the country.

Planes create noise pollution, especially when they have to come in low over residential areas, such as this one coming in to land over the highrises of Hong Kong.

CONGESTED CITIES

Many historic towns and cities, including Athens, Rome and London, suffer from serious traffic congestion and air pollution. The air pollution creates acid rain, which damages buildings and statues. Tourists hire cars, which adds to the congestion. Tourists can help by choosing to use public transport, walking, or hiring bikes to see the sights.

The affect of air pollution can be seen in many ways. Ancient buildings, such as the Acropolis in Greece, gradually crumble away.

'Governments should develop and promote cost-effective, more efficient, less polluting and safer transport systems as well as environmentally sound road networks.'

AGENDA 21

WALKING AND CYCLING

Walking has long been a popular activity in the Alps, and there are many lovely paths through the mountains. Walking maps show the paths marked according to their level of difficulty.

Walking holidays are very popular. They are not only fun, but, as long people dispose of their rubbish carefully and keep to the paths, they are also environmentally sensitive.

Many holiday areas now encourage people to get out into the countryside by bike. There are centres where people can hire bikes and buy maps that show routes that are good for cycling. Not only is this a pollution-free mode of transport, but visitors get to see much more of the countryside.

Why not get fit as you see the sights, like these cyclists who are touring the South Island, New Zealand?

CASE STUDY

ZERMATT, SWITZERLAND

A CAR-FREE VILLAGE

Zermatt is a picture-postcard village in the Swiss Alps, nestling under the Matterhorn. Its streets are narrow and not suited to cars. Many years ago, Zermatt decided to ban cars and lorries. Visitors to the town have to leave their cars lower down the valley and complete their journey by train. On arrival at the station, they are transported to their hotel or chalet by special carts which are either pulled by horse or powered by electric engines. This leaves the streets free of traffic, so people can wander around quite safely, with no noise or pollution.

Many hotels in Zermatt have their own horse-drawn taxis.

AGENDA 21 aims to:

- reduce water pollution
- save water
- clean up the beaches
- build more attractive resorts

BEACH HOLIDAYS

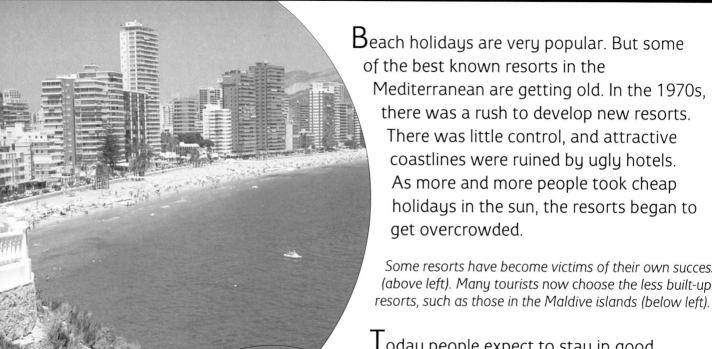

Beach holidays are very popular. But some of the best known resorts in the Mediterranean are getting old. In the 1970s, there was a rush to develop new resorts. There was little control, and attractive coastlines were ruined by ugly hotels. As more and more people took cheap holidays in the sun, the resorts began to get overcrowded.

Some resorts have become victims of their own success (above left). Many tourists now choose the less built-up resorts, such as those in the Maldive islands (below left).

Today people expect to stay in good hotels with swimming pools, eat well-prepared food and swim in clean water. The Mediterranean resorts are losing business to the new resorts in exotic locations, such as the Caribbean and Far East. In an attempt to bring back the tourists, Mediterranean resorts are redesigning themselves. The new developments blend with local environment and use traditional materials.

WHERE DOES THE WASTE GO?

In the past, there were few environmental controls. Hotels were often built in places which did not have sewage treatment plants, so untreated sewage and waste water was emptied straight into the sea. Raw sewage contains bacteria, and this makes the water unfit for swimming.

In many tourist areas around the world, untreated waste water is fed into the sea. This poses a health risk, particularly for people who visit the beaches to bathe.

As the number of tourists increases, so does the amount of sewage. Holiday brochures show pictures of hotels beside idyllic bays, but they do not indicate that the water may be polluted. In Europe, the blue flag scheme now helps tourists to find the cleanest beaches. The water in the sea has to be tested regularly throughout the year. If the water is clean enough, the resort is awarded a blue flag.

Sandbanks' beach, in Dorset in the UK, has become renowned for its clean beach and water, so proudly flies its blue flag.

RUNNING OUT OF WATER

The Mediterranean has a dry climate. The rain falls mainly during the cooler winter months, but the water has to last all summer. As the number of tourists increases, so does the demand for water – for showers, cooking, cleaning and for filling swimming pools.

Over the last 10 years, the fresh water reserves of the Mediterranean countries have fallen, and there are water shortages in summer. To overcome this problem, resorts may have to limit the number of tourists. The tourists who do use the resort must conserve water. Also, as much water as possible has to be trapped during the winter and stored for use during the summer.

In some resorts, water is carefully recycled. Waste water is used to water the plants and shrubs around the complex.

CASE STUDY

FLORIDA, USA

FLORIDA – THE SUNSHINE STATE

Florida is the holiday state of the USA. Millions of visitors from around the world travel to 'the sunshine state' for the weather, the theme parks and the Everglades. But the environment is suffering.

The Everglades is a huge area of marsh which is home to millions of birds and other animals. But, as the holiday resorts, theme parks and golf courses use more water, the marshes are drying up. The water that remains is being polluted by sewage and fertilizers from agricultural land. The coral reefs off the coast are also dying because of the water pollution.

Now, the state government is looking at ways of saving water and conserving the natural habitats which form the highlight of many people's holidays.

(Above) Tourists learn about the wildlife of the Everglades and the Florida Keys (right). Awareness is a big part of conservation.

LOOKING AFTER HISTORIC SITES

People love visiting historic sites such as the Acropolis in Athens, Stonehenge in England, and the pyramids in Egypt. By visiting these sites they learn about the past.

Historic sites need visitors. It is a constant battle to keep old buildings and monuments in good condition – this costs a lot of money. The entrance fees help to pay for the upkeep of the site. But visitors also create problems and cause damage.

Everyday, thousands of pairs of feet wear out paths, lawns, carpets and floors. People may drop litter at the site and some people even write graffiti on the walls and stones. As a result, many sites are closed to the public for conservation reasons. For example, in order to protect the prehistoric stones at Stonehenge, in the UK, visitors are now prevented from touching or walking near them.

Once it was possible to walk among the stones at Stonehenge. Due to acts of vandalism, however, it is now protected by a fence and it is no longer possible for visitors to see the stones close up.

ATTACK FROM THE AIR

Many historic sites are also under attack from air pollution. Car fumes and factory emissions generated in towns and cities cause pollution that blackens stone buildings. Acid rain can eat away limestone rock and completely destroy the features on statues.

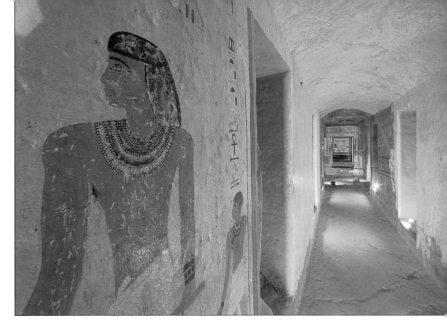

(Above) Moisture released into the air from people breathing and sweating damages the paintings inside the tombs. The number of visitors needs to be limited (left).

The traffic-congested streets of Cairo, Egypt, create a smog that lies over the city. Nearby, the world-famous pyramids are being seriously damaged by the city's air pollution. The pyramids are very popular and are visited by thousands of people each day. At one time, people could climb the pyramids, crawl over the Sphinx, and collect rock as a souvenir.

(Below) The smog rising above the city of Cairo, drifts across to affect the stones of the pyramids at Giza.

Fortunately, there is now more control. People are allowed to enter the pyramids to see the tombs inside, but they must be accompanied by an official guide. Flashlight photography is not permitted because it damages the ancient paintings on the walls of the tomb.

MANAGING NUMBERS

In 1994, almost three million people visited the historic university city of Cambridge in the UK. In 2001, more than four million visitors are expected, so the city is planning for the future.

Visitors bring in a lot of money which benefits the local economy. Some of this money will be spent on the city, conserving the buildings to make sure that visitors continue to visit. But the narrow city streets quickly become congested. The city has plans to reduce congestion by charging people to use the city's roads. This will not only preserve the town's historical buildings by cutting down pollution, but will also help tourists to move around the city more easily and have a better experience.

Cambridge does not need to attract visitors, instead it has to learn to manage them in a sustainable way.

FINDING A BALANCE

There has to be a balance between the number of visitors allowed to a site of interest, the money they bring in, and the conservation of the site itself. Sometimes it is necessary to charge visitors more. This way there are fewer visitors, but the income remains the same. Another way is to limit the number of visitors, perhaps by only allowing so many to enter each day.

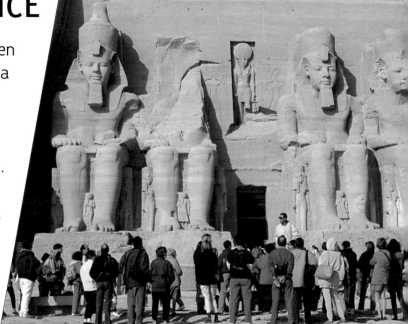

Managing visitors is the key to ecotourism.

ATHENS, GREECE

PROTECTING ANCIENT SITES

23

Athens has many famous archaeological sites, most of which are of international importance, so they have to be preserved and protected. But these sites are scattered throughout the city and are surrounded by buildings and roads. They are being damaged by air pollution. Tourists find travelling from one site to another very difficult because the city suffers from traffic congestion.

Athens is now planning to link the sites with a 700 hectare archaeological park stretching through the heart of the city. The sites will be surrounded by green open spaces, so they will look more attractive and be more interesting to visit. Money will be spent improving some of the run-down buildings near the sites, and on reducing traffic congestion and air pollution.

(Above and right) To protect the Parthenon from the pollution of Athens, a 'bubble' may be constructed around it.

WILDLIFE HOLIDAYS

Many people enjoy watching wildlife. They travel to East Africa to go on safari, or visit the jungles of South America and Southeast Asia. They get a thrill from seeing wildlife close-up, such as a pride of lions around a kill, or the mystifying mountain gorilla. But there is a problem of balance. The tourists bring in money, but too many tourists can also damage the environment.

Managed groups of people can pay to see the endangered mountain gorillas. The money raised is used to protect the animals and support the local economy.

ON SAFARI

Kenya is a popular destination for safari holidays, but it has been almost too successful. Tourism is Kenya's number one industry. In 1994, just under one million tourists visited the national parks. The money raised from these visits supports the Kenyan Wildlife Service. But the number of tourists is putting severe pressure on resources such as water. And the animals are suffering, too.

Many animals in game reserves are used to tourist vehicles, and even climb aboard to get a better view!

Everybody wants to see the 'big five' animals – lions, cheetahs, leopards, elephants and rhinos. These animals are followed by buses full of tourists with video cameras, trying to capture the moment of the kill. They often disturb the hunt, causing the lioness or cheetah to miss their prey.

(Above) Although exciting, it is not always fair on the animals to get close to the kill.

CASE STUDY

ZIMBABWE, AFRICA

BIG GAME HUNTING

Conservation is all about protecting wildlife, so it seems strange that allowing people to shoot some animals could actually help. But in Zimbabwe, the conservation of the elephant has been so successful that, in some parks, there are too many elephants. Their numbers have to be controlled in order to stop them from ruining their own habitat. Rich people will pay a lot of money to be able to shoot a large animal, such as a buffalo or elephant. Big game hunting is one way in which tourism can be made to pay for a lot of conservation.

Now the poaching of elephants for their ivory has lessened, their numbers are increasing. But their population needs to be controlled because they damage the habitat for themselves and other animals.

COLOURFUL CORAL REEFS

Coral reefs are found in clear, warm, tropical waters. They are full of marine life and very popular with divers. Many people learn how to dive on holiday. But coral reefs are very fragile environments. They are being harmed by hotel building, diving and sailing.

Building work releases sand which settles over the reef killing the coral. The beach hotels release sewage and other pollution into the sea. Pleasure boats take people to the reef, and anchors are let down which damage the coral. Divers and snorkellers disturb the fish and touch the coral. Some break off the coral as a souvenir.

'One of the key things is getting information to tourists. For example if you know that coral is a living animal you might not want to touch it.'

Dr David Righton of Frontier, a reef conservation organization.

CASE STUDY

GREAT BARRIER REEF, AUSTRALIA

OFF-LIMIT ZONES

The Great Barrier Reef is great for diving. In an attempt to preserve the reef and keep it in an unspoilt state, the Australian authorities have divided the reef into zones. The public may enter some zones and explore the reef, but other areas are off limits and the reef is left undisturbed. Public zones have special anchor points to stop the boats from damaging the reef.

Divers must follow a code of conduct when they dive, so that all divers can enjoy the beauty of the coral reef.

HELPING CONSERVATION

Many of the wildlife tour operators understand that their business depends on the survival and well-being of the wildlife they take people to see. Some operators give money to conservation projects. Wildlife Tours in Costa Rica, for example, supports projects to conserve rare turtles and monkeys.

'Antarctica has become so popular with sightseers that scientists have had to devise a way to protect penguins from tourist-induced stress.'

Carole Cadwalladr, travel journalist.

Earthwatch is a conservation charity that allows people to pay to join a real research project. Visitors might opt to pay to work with orphaned orang-utans in Borneo.

THE LAST WILDERNESS?

Wildlife holidays are popular. But if too many people are allowed into wilderness areas, or to enter national parks, the wildlife will suffer. One of the latest destinations is Antarctica. Tourist numbers have exploded, from just a few hundred in 1990, to more than 10,000 in 1996. Great care has to be taken, for this fragile polar habitat is very easily damaged. Antarctica is the last great unspoilt wilderness and, somehow, we have to make sure that it stays that way.

The pristine home of the emperor penguins, beneath the ice cliffs of Antarctica.

AGENDA 21 aims to:

- encourage people to choose tour operators who care about the environment
- ensure people act responsibly when on holiday

Clearing rubbish at base camp, the Himalayas.

CHOOSING A HOLIDAY

'Everything you go to see is changed by the very action of going to see it.'

Douglas Adams, author.

So how can you help? Everybody makes choices when they select a holiday. You can help your family to choose wisely. Before you travel, find out about your holiday destination. Learn about its history, culture, language and natural environment. Ask the tour operator questions about your chosen hotel. For example, are the hotel staff local people or are they hired in other countries? Does the operator donate money to local conservation projects?

When choosing a holiday, it is useful to find out how environmentally aware the resort that you would like to visit is.

TOURISM AND MONEY

Tourism is about money, and money means power. Some of the largest tour operators have a lot of power. They can persuade a government to let them build new resorts and facilities. But their customers hold the real power. You can refuse to go on holidays which cause damage.

Some of the better operators will support local communities by giving the jobs to local people. They make sure that tourists pay a fair price for local crafts, such as pottery, and they encourage people to learn about the place they are visiting.

'Take nothing but photographs, leave nothing but footprints.'

THE FUTURE

Fortunately, many places in the world are still remote and unspoilt. But, if we are not careful, they too will be damaged. The only way that they will remain unspoilt is to restrict the number of people who visit them, and minimize the impact of those who do. It would be a shame to have to ban people from beautiful or interesting places altogether.

29

From the coast of Tahiti (left) to the eastern tip of Australia (above), there are many unspoilt parts of the world that we need to respect and preserve.

GLOSSARY

acid rain: an acidic rain that forms when sulphur from smoke mixes with water droplets in the air.

archaeological site: a place where the remains of an ancient settlement have been discovered.

conservation: the preservation and protection of wildlife and habitats.

culture: a country's way of life, customs and traditions.

development: a stage of growth or advancement.

environment: the natural world that surrounds us, including the air, the soil, water and other animals and plants.

exotic: an unusual or tropical location overseas.

fertilizer: a substance containing nutrients necessary for healthy plant growth.

Grand Tour: a tour of main cities and places of interest, usually within Europe. In the past, it was considered an important part of someone's education.

habitat: the living area of a plant or animal, for example a pond or a wood.

heritage: in this case, a country's historic buildings, monuments and natural landscape.

historical: belonging to the past.

package holiday: a ready made holiday, with accommodation and transport prearranged, that you choose from a brochure.

pilgrim: a person who travels to a sacred place for religious reasons.

polar: to do with the North or South Pole.

poaching: the illegal killing of an animal in order to eat it or in order to take its skin or tusks to sell.

pollution: harmful substances in the air, water or ground.

renewable: something that can be replaced or regrown, for example trees; or a source of energy that never runs out, such as the sun or wind.

resort: a holiday village or town.

safari: a holiday on which you visit game reserves to watch wildlife.

sewage: the waste from toilets which is carried away in the drains.

spa: a place where people can bathe in healthy mineral waters.

sustainable: in this instance, to be able to maintain lifestyles or preserve resources over a long period of time.

FURTHER INFORMATION

Earthwatch
Belsyre Court
Observatory Road
Oxford OX2 6HU, UK
Tel: 01865 516366

Friends of the Earth
26-28 Underwood Street
London, N1 7JQ, UK
Tel: 0171 490 1555
(Website http://www.foe.org)

International Council for Local Environmental Initiatives (ICLEI)
(Website http://www.iclei.org)

Tourism Concern
Froebel College
Roehampton Lane
London, SW15 5PJ, UK
Tel: 0181 392 3000

Worldwide Fund for Nature
Panda House
Weyside Park
Godalming
Surrey GU7 1XR, UK
Tel: 01483 426444
(Website http://www.panda.org)

Earthcare
1027 Mountain Highway
Bayswater VIC 3153
AUSTRALIA
Free call: 1800 335 508

Friends of the Earth
Suite 15/104 Bathurst Street
Sydney NSW 2000
AUSTRALIA
Tel: 9283 2004

Tourism Council Australia
Level 2/80 William Street
Woolloomooloo NSW 2029
AUSTRALIA
Tel: 9360 3500

Worldwide Fund for Nature
Level 1/17 York Street
Sydney NSW 2000
AUSTRALIA
Tel: 9299 6366

INDEX